Winter Whimsy

by Mary Jo Huff
illustrated by Jerry Jindrich

Dedication

This book is dedicated to all the people who have listened as I shared my stories. To my husband Bill who makes this crazy life I lead make sense. To my mama Sissy, who quilts from one season to another, and leaves her story in her stitches. For my children, Cathy, Kenny, Joe, Nikki, Melody and John, and their patience when I had to fly off to another adventure.

A special thanks and a big hug to my grandchildren, Kurt, Melanie, Matthew and Michael who are the lights in the darkness of this world. A special thanks to Susan and Jerry Jindrich who encourage and draw stories for all children. To Carol and my sister Connie who always listens and to the "CUZ" connection that keeps our family stories alive.

We are responsible for handing down the past to the present and preserving the present for the future by telling our story.

This book is dedicated to
All the storytellers in the world and for all the young to-be-storytellers who are ready to share a story!

Publisher: Roberta Suid

Production: Little Acorn & Associates, Inc.

WINTER WHIMSY

For a complete catalog, write to the address below:
Monday Morning Books, Inc.
PO Box 1134
Inverness, CA 94937

Call our toll-free number: 1-800-255-6049
E-mail us at: MMBooks@aol.com
Visit our Web site:
http://www.mondaymorningbooks.com

ISBN 1-57612-180-1

Printed in the United States of America
9 8 7 6 5 4 3 2 1

Contents

Introduction

The *Winter Whimsy* book is one in a series of seasonal books. It is designed to accompany the *Spring Fling*, *Summer Surprise* and *Fall Frolic* books. A main focus of this book is to provide a vehicle for children to use language and have fun with puppets.

Language fluency can be increased through storytelling. Stories can be changed to make them more interesting to children. This can be accomplished by telling familiar stories (such as the "Three Pigs," "Three Bears," and "Three Billy Goats Gruff") with updated ideas.

This book can be used in several ways by different classroom levels.

- Teachers can use stories and puppet patterns with children.
- Children can create puppets to go with their favorite stories.
- Children can write their own stories and tell them using a puppet.

Provide a special area in the classroom for the children to gather and retell stories. This area should be equipped with many tools. Invite the children to bring items from home and place them in a basket or box for retelling at special assigned times.

Equip this special area with tools such as:

- Books
- Musical instruments
- Tape recorder
- Storyboard
- Puppets
- Storytelling aprons
- Story characters
- Writing materials
- Story bags
- Story sheets
- Story boxes

Give children the time and opportunity so their stories can be documented with video, tape recorders, cameras or journals. Storytelling is truly a literacy connection.

Family Fun is a connection between the classroom and the home. Children are encouraged to take home ideas and projects that extend the learning process. Ideas are provided to help teachers with this connection. Provide adequate information for the children and parents to interact with language, science, math and literacy projects.

Storytelling Hints

- Your Own Words - There is no right or wrong way to tell a story. Tell the story your way and do not try to memorize the words. Let the story flow and enjoy the response.

- Eye Contact - Make good eye contact when telling stories to an audience.

- Voice - Let your voice express the special points in a story. Voice changes are fun for the listener.

- Body Language - Let your body move with the story. Don't over use the body but let it move naturally with the story.

- Audience Participation - Let the audience in on the fun and invite them to help with your story. When a story has a repetitive element such as "Run, run as fast as you can," let the audience enjoy repeating these words.

When children are engaged in a meaningful, developmentally appropriate experience like storytelling, they become interested in reading, writing, speaking, listening and problem solving. All children do not learn the same way and storytelling opens up many new areas for teaching.

Storytelling Hints

Benefits of Storytelling as an Educational Tool

- Improves and Develops Language Skills: Reading, Writing, Listening, Speaking
- Motivates Students to Learn
- Is a Cross-curriculum Tool
- Develops Creative Imagination
- Improves Problem Solving Skills
- Creates a Connection to Community, Family, and Friends
- Engages and Entertains

Storytelling Can Be Used For

- Education
- Motivation
- Business
- Healing
- Youth
- Adults
- Communities
- History Connections
- Fun

Storytelling Hints

Set up an area where children want to use and share language. Provide soft chairs, a couch, bean bags, a rocking chair, a small table, and chairs, book shelves filled with books, puppets and a special STORY WALL.

Create a STORY WALL by covering an area with Velcro material and adding a seasonal border. Take the time to prepare the things you will use on this wall. Many ideas in seasonal books can be adapted for the story wall.

The STORY WALL is similar to a word wall. Take a story that you are preparing to read or tell to the children and pick out the special words you want them to use. Type these words on a computer, laminate the words and attach a small piece of Velcro hook to the back. Colored copies of pictures from the story can also be laminated and used on the story wall.

Children can learn about characters, settings, titles, authors or any part of a story you choose to prepare.

Put each story in a plastic envelope from the local office store and file them in a crate so children are free to choose a story and retell it using the story words and pictures on the story wall. Label the envelopes and children will begin reading the titles.

Change the stories in the crate as the seasons change. The children will be exposed to new and different language. They will share this language with others as they retell the stories.

This wall can be used for any special event and can highlight birthdays or any other child centered activity. Be creative and use recycled books, magazines, children's art, art foam characters and flannel board characters to add to the visual effect of telling a story.

STORY WALL

Storytelling Tool Box

Materials:

Toolbox (purchase at local hardware story)
Musical Instruments
Scarves
Story Wand
Rubber Fingernails
Masks
Small Puppets

How To

Collect items throughout the year and add to the toolbox. Puppets and props concealed in the toolbox add a little mystery to your storytime.

Kid Fun

Children enjoy trying to guess what is new in the toolbox. The storyteller can give clues and let the children guess. They also look forward to each time the toolbox is opened. Children can bring story items from home to share with other children.

Family Fun

A fun parent and child activity is to create a story box at home. A shoe box that is decorated by the child and parent can be a special story box that items are added to throughout the child's young life. It is also a wonderful keepsake box.

Literacy Connections

Story Maps

Journals

Show and Tell

Overhead Projector Stories

Word Wheels

Word Walls

Daily News Report

Alphabet Books

Flap Books

Storyboard

Storyboard Stories

Story Gloves

Story Basket

Mascot

Puppets and Puppet Houses

My Winter Story

In the winter I like to ______________________________.

In the winter I like to eat______________________________.

My favorite thing about winter is ____________________

____.

This is me in the winter.

Kid Fun

The children can fill in the blanks and this story can be sent home for the family to read.

Family Fun

The family can take this beginning and write their own winter story.

Mascot

Meet Mr. Mascot, he is a lovable, creative teaching tool. Varmint is my favorite mascot puppet. He is a PUPPET and he lives in a house! His house is a basket painted with doors, windows, bushes and a red roof.

I encourage you to find a puppet you can work with and use the puppet in your year-round seasonal curriculum.

Let your mascot have a wardrobe that has been collected over time. His winter wardrobe consists of:

- a jacket
- a hat
- gloves
- a scarf
- a small shovel for snow
- winter puppet friends

Mascot

My mascot is active in every aspect of the curriculum and springs many surprises. Think how you could put a puppet to use everyday. Let your mascot puppet:

- Do a morning greeting
- Say hello in different languages
- Do the weather report
- Write notes to the teacher or children
- Explain the daily activities
- Introduce visitors

The mascot can also visit with parents at an open house or special time when the parents visit. A puppet can convey many messages that may be troublesome for you. He can express the importance of parent involvement with their children.

On a special reading night, the mascot puppet can read to the children and adults.

The mascot can go along on field trips and carry a first aid kit in a backpack. He can be the rule setter and leader on the trip.

The puppet can wear a costume from other countries and become a global connection to other areas of our world.

Seasons

(Sing to Always)

May there always be Winter
May there always be Spring

May there always be Summer
May there always be Autumn

May there always be Children
May there always be Stories

May there always be Seasons
May there always be Love!

Season Verse

I looked out my window and what did I see? (hands over eyes)
The world was changing in front of me.

I looked out my window and what did I see? (hands over eyes)
Snow was falling from the sky for me.
(slowly wiggle fingers and let the snow fall)

Snow, snow was falling
Snow, snow was falling
Snow, snow was falling
Snow was falling for the world to see.

I looked out my window and what did I see? (hands over eyes)
The world was changing in front of me.

I looked out my window and what did I see? (cup hands over eyes)
Spring flowers blooming for you and me. (lift arms and hands up in the air)

Spring flowers, spring flowers blooming.
Spring flowers, spring flowers blooming.
Spring flowers, spring flowers blooming.
Spring flowers a blooming for the world to see.

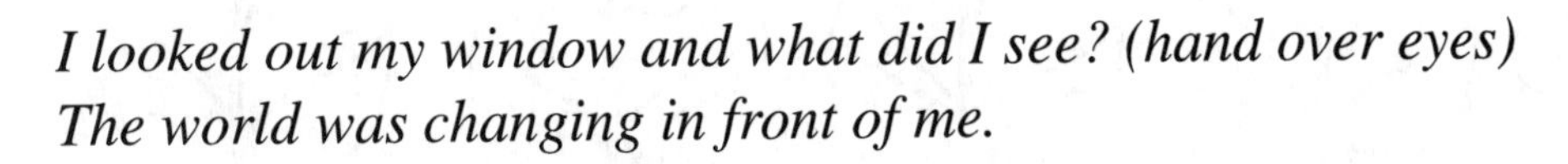

I looked out my window and what did I see? (hand over eyes)
The world was changing in front of me.

I looked out my window and what did I see? (hand over eyes)
Summer sunshine for you and me.
(circle arms over head)

Season Verse

Sunshine, summer sunshine
Sunshine, summer sunshine
Sunshine, summer sunshine
Summer sunshine for the world to see.

I looked out my window and what did I see?
The world was changing in front of me. (hand over eyes)

I looked out my window and what did I see? (hand over eyes)
Leaves were falling from the trees by me. (hands drift from the sky)

Colors, colors falling
Colors, colors falling
Colors, colors falling
Colored leaves falling for the world to see.

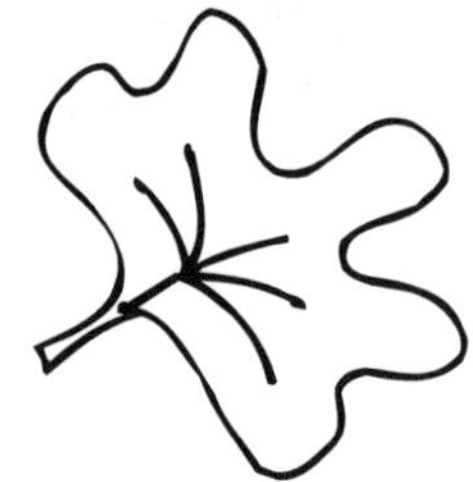

Sing the verse that goes with the season and add a season as the year progresses.

Kid Fun

Create a seasonal bulletin board and let the children add the colored leaves in the fall, the snow in winter, the flowers in spring and the sunshine in the summer.

Velcro Connections

Velcro is a powerful tool for anyone who works with children. Velcro-type storyboards are much easier to use than the old type of flannel boards. Items placed on the storyboards do not fall off and children can manipulate the story characters easily.

Ideas

Storyboard – Cover a masonite board (this can be purchased from a local hardware store) with Velcro-type loop fabric. Cut the fabric wider and longer than the board and attach the Velcro-type loop material to the back of the board with duct tape. This board can be attached to a wall or set up on a tripod for use. There are many different ways to make a storyboard but this is the simplest way.

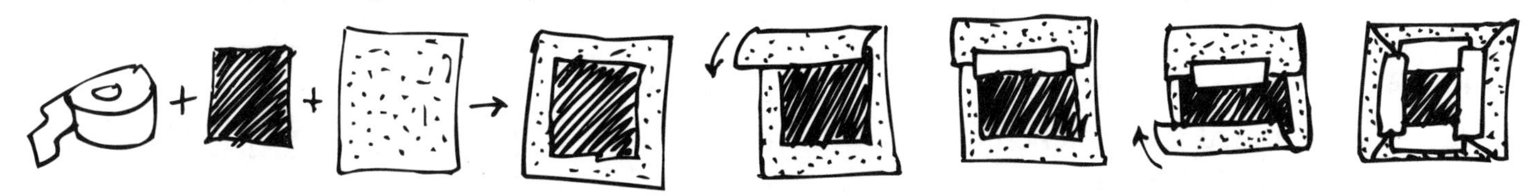

Story Bands – Story bands can be cut from the loop fabric. Cut the long story band strip in half for children. Two story bands come from one width of material. Attach a piece of self-adhesive Velcro hook to the back side of the bands.

Slide the story bands under the children's arms and attach in the back. Add any story character and they are ready for a dramatic event. Patterns in this book can be used for story characters. Use heavy poster board or art foam to make your characters. Attach a small piece of the Velcro hook to each character and you are ready for storytime.

Velcro Connections

Story Boxes – Any kind of box with a lid (pizza boxes and shoe boxes are great) will work. Attach a piece of Velcro loop fabric to the lid. The material can be attached to the lid with E-6000 glue. It must be completely dry before using. Create story characters and attach a small piece of Velcro hook to the back and you are ready to tell story box stories.

These boxes are great to send home with the children. Stories can be added to the boxes to become a family-school connection. Story boxes can be used like private little word walls. The children can place pictures and/or words in their boxes and take them home to interact with family storytelling and word recognition.

Story Walls = Word Walls. The Velcro fabric can be cut to any size, hemmed and attached to a wall to create a fabulous word wall. Story pictures and story words can be placed on this wall for the children to see at all times.

Suddenly the word wall becomes a story wall and the children can retell their stories just using the pictures and/or words from the story.

Velcro Story Apron – An apron can be purchased from one of the listed suppliers in the back of the book or you can sew your own. The storytelling apron is a handy tool for all educators. The Velcro loop fabric creates a moving storyboard and items can be placed in the pockets. This type of apron can be used in all areas of the curriculum and most of the characters are created from art foam, from magazines or from household items. Velcro hook must be added to the back of anything that is used to stick on the apron.

The apron can be used for:

- Storytelling
- Sequencing
- Matching
- Math
- Science
- Social Studies
- Announcements

Story Sample

Who — Acorn
What — Weather Changed
When — Early Winter
Where — In the Woods
Why — Wind Blew the Acorn to the Ground

Materials:

Velcro storyboard
Velcro hook
Green art foam
Light brown art foam
Dark brown art foam

Directions:

Copy the patterns on the following pages, cut out patterns and attach a small piece of Velcro hook. Add pieces to the storyboard as you tell the story of the wind blowing the little acorn from the tree.

Kid Fun

Let the children place the art foam on the storyboard as you tell the story. This type of story can be available in the story area for the children to retell the story in their own words.

Little Acorn Story

Once upon a day before yesterday there was a tall mountain that had many, many trees on its slopes. The trees grew tall and sturdy in the fresh mountain air. One wintry day a strong wind blew through the timbers and many of the trees lost their leaves, acorns and even some small branches.

When a tiny acorn falls to the ground it could be lost forever. The winter is a quiet time in the forest and the little acorn lies still and quiet on the ground. In the spring as the sun breaks through the timbers, the wind blows and the rain comes down, the little acorn begins to change.

The warmth of the sun and the wet of the spring rain help the little acorn begin to sprout. And as that little acorn begins to sprout he lifts his new leaves up towards the sun and feels the gentle breeze inviting him to grow taller and taller.

Someday this little acorn will be a tall, sturdy tree growing on the slopes of the mountain where his father and his grandfather grew. There is an old saying, "The acorn never falls very far from the tree."

Just like that acorn, we may grow up like our fathers and grandfathers before us because we are the acorns of their trees.

Directions:

Create the storytelling props. Patterns can be copied and placed on the art foam and then cut out. Use your imagination to fill in the creative lines. Marker or acrylic paint can be used on this type of prop. The story can be placed on a storyboard and children can use the board for story retelling.

Acorn Story Patterns

Acorn Story Patterns

Acorn Story Patterns

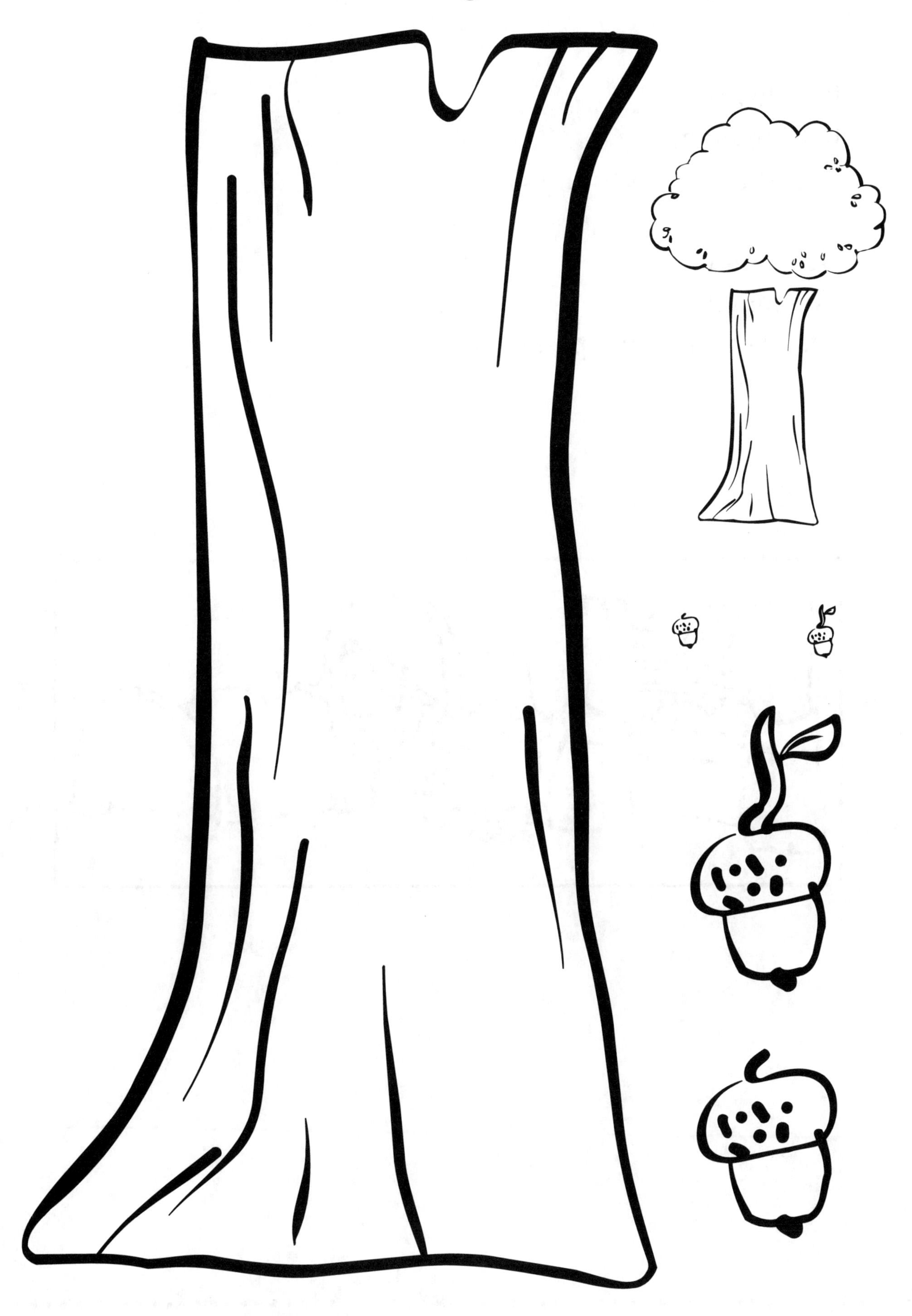

Winter Whimsy

It's blowing.
It's snowing.
The old man is snoring.

He went to bed and
Covered his head
And wouldn't get up this morning.

Bear Hunt

(This is a call back.)

We are going on a bear hunt.
Pack a backpack full of stuff you
might need on a hike in the woods.
(Children choose items to put in the backpack, but always make sure there is
a flashlight.)

Going on a bear hunt!
Going on a bear hunt!
Going to find a bear!
Going to find a bear!

A big ole bear
A big ole bear
With a giant grooowwwl
With a giant grooowwwl
And a stumpy tail.
And a stumpy tail.

Oh look
Oh look
Over there.
Over there.
It's a lagoon.
It's a lagoon.
It's a lollipop lagoon.
It's a lollipop lagoon.

Can't go over it.
Can't go over it.
Can't go under it.
Can't go under it.
Can't go around it.
Can't go around it.

Have to lick our way across it.
Have to lick our way across it.
Lick, Lick, Lick.
Lick, Lick, Lick.

Going on a bear hunt!
Going on a bear hunt!
Going to find a bear!
Going to find a bear!

A big ole bear
A big ole bear
With a giant grooowwwl
With a giant grooowwwl
And a stumpy tail.
And a stumpy tail.

Oh look
Oh look
Over there.
Over there.
It's a swamp.
It's a swamp.
A marshmallow swamp.
A marshmallow swamp.

Bear Hunt

Can't go over it.
Can't go over it.
Can't go under it.
Can't go under it.
Can't go around it.
Can't go around it.
Have to go across it.
Have to go across it.

Wibble, Wobble, Wibble, Wobble.
Wibble, Wobble, Wibble, Wobble.

Going on a bear hunt!
Going on a bear hunt!
Going to find a bear!
Going to find a bear!

A big ole bear
A big ole bear
With a giant grooowwwl
With a giant grooowwwl
And a stumpy tail.
And a stumpy tail.

Oh look
Oh look
Over there.
Over there.
It's a woods, a big dark woods.
It's a woods, a big dark woods.

Can't go over it.
Can't go over it.
Can't go under it.
Can't go under it.
Can't go around it.
Can't go around it.
We'll have to go through it.
We'll have to go through it.

OOOOOOOOOOO
OOOOOOOOOOO
It's scary in the woods!
It's scary in the woods!

Going on a bear hunt!
Going on a bear hunt!
Going to find a bear!
Going to find a bear!

A big ole bear
A big ole bear
With a giant grooowwwl
With a giant grooowwwl
And a stumpy tail.
And a stumpy tail.

Bear Hunt

Oh look
Oh look
Over there.
Over there.
It's a cave.
It's a cave.
A dark, dark cave.
A dark, dark cave.

Can't go over it.
Can't go over it.
Can't go under it.
Can't go under it.
Can't go around it.
Can't go around it.
We'll have to go in it.
We'll have to go in it.

Tiptoe, Tiptoe, Tiptoe.
Tiptoe, Tiptoe, Tiptoe.

I smell something.
I smell something. ***(smell)***
I hear something.
I hear something. ***(listen)***
It's Snoring!
It's Snoring!

It's really dark in here. Let's open our backpacks and get out our flashlights. Count one, two, three, and we will turn on our flashlights.

One, two, three, Click.
Ohhhhhh, No!
It's a bear!!!
It's a bear!!!
Runnnnnnn!

Back through the dark woods,
Back through the marshmallow swamp,
Back across the lollipop lagoon,
and runnnnn for home.

Go inside and lock the door.
Oh no! We forgot something.
Do you know what it could be?
The backpack... I'm not going to go back, are you?

Snow

Snow, snow, I saw snow
Snow, snow, I saw snow
Snow, snow, I saw snow
I saw snow in the sky.

Soft and white falling down,
Covering everything in our town.

Snow, snow, I saw snow
Snow, snow, I saw snow
Snow, snow, I saw snow
I saw snow, in the sky.

Cold and wet on the ground,
Helps me make a snowman round.

Snow, snow, I saw snow
Snow, snow, I saw snow
Snow, snow, I saw snow
I love snow from the sky.

Five Little Snowmen

(chant)

Five little snowmen
Standing in a row

The wind blew hard and one had to go.

Four little snowmen
Standing in a row

The rain came down and one had to go.

Three little snowmen
Standing in a row

Along came a snowplow and one had to go.

Two little snowmen
Standing in a row

Waiting for children but one had to go.

One little snowman
Standing in a row

The sun came out and
No more snowmen standing in a row.

Jug Puppets

Creating a puppet from a gallon or half-gallon plastic jug is an economical way to provide many children with a puppet character to accompany a good story. Some jugs contain drinking water, distilled water, milk, juice or unused jugs can be found at a local milk company. Some milk companies will donate jugs for a project. We are helping the Earth by using recyclable materials like the plastic jugs. Children can use their imaginations to create and decorate a puppet. They can tell, retell or write a story to accompany the puppet.

Materials:

- A clean plastic jug - gallon or half-gallon
- Sharp scissors (for adult use only)
- Tape
- Avery markers (These are the markers that work best on the plastic.) They come in many colors and as highlighters. The highlighters give the puppets a brighter color and some will glow in the dark. Purchase these markers at local office supply stores. Crafty Dab paint can also be purchased at local craft stores. This paint is designed to stick to plastic and not crack off.

Make a copy of the original jug pattern and cut out the pattern.

Handle

The handle of the jug is what the children hold onto when using the jug to tell a story, sing a song, or march in a parade or just having fun.

How To

Wash the plastic jug thoroughly and fill the jug with hot water. Let the hot water sit inside the jug for several minutes and then peel off the label. If you have difficulty, try some Goo Gone from your local discount store. Only adults should use this glue remover.

Jug Puppets

Directions for most jugs:

Cut off the small top where the lid screws on (the spout).

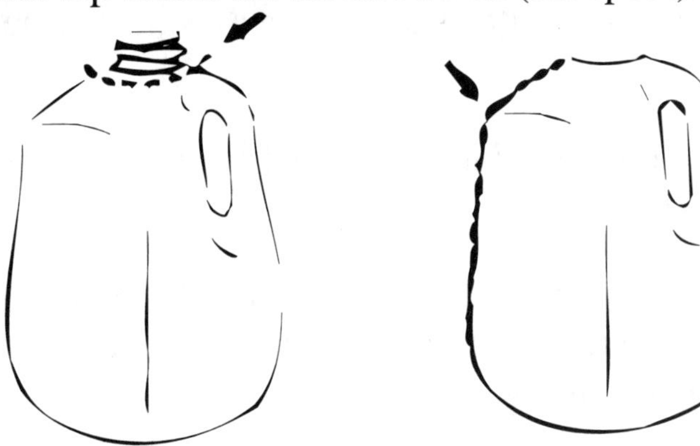

Cut down the middle on the opposite side of the handle to open the jug.

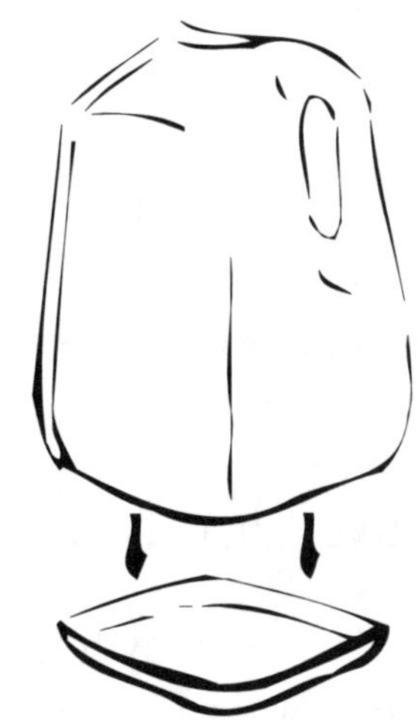

Cut away the bottom of the jug.

Review pattern directions to see if the bottom is needed to create your puppet. A few patterns may need the bottom of the jug for the character.

Tape pattern A to one side of the jug handle and pattern B on the other side of the handle. Patterns should be placed at the top of the jug first. Trace the pattern with a black permanent marker then remove the paper pattern and cut out the puppet on the traced lines.

Or tape pattern A on one side of the jug handle and pattern B on the other side of the handle. Cut around the paper pattern without tracing. Some patterns may have to be adjusted according to the contour of the jug. Use your judgment on the pattern. Decorate the jug puppet to suit your story and add the features such as eyes, mouth, hair, etc.

Jug Puppets

When the pattern is on the jug and you see an excess of plastic (plastic outside the pattern line or pattern) cut it away before trying to cut out the puppet. Save your plastic scraps and cut shapes or other items and put in a literacy center or an art center.

Test your jug to see if the marker or paint looks better on the inside or the outside of the jug. Plastic varies from state to state.

Attach a piece of rope to the ceiling of your classroom and attach the jugs to the string with clothespins for storage. A clothes line can also be attached to the walls and jugs attached to this line for storage.

Note: Always complete the pattern at TOP and BOTTOM of the jug where the paper pattern does not meet.

Kid Fun

The children can use the Avery markers or Crafty Dab paint to create a rainbow of colors for their jug puppet. This is a free art experience and hands-on activity that can be repeated throughout the year. The puppets can be sent home or used in a story area at school.

Let the children be creative. There is no right and wrong way to do this project.

Scraps of leftover plastic can be recycled. Cut the leftover plastic in any design; add color with the markers, punch a hole and string the pieces and hang in a window or from the ceiling.

Family Fun

Send your families the instructions and patterns for the puppets. The children and their family members can cut out different kinds of puppets to use with storytelling and story retelling. They can make puppets to represent the members of their family and tell their story. Parents can help the children make puppets and write special stories for the class. This is a great connection between classroom and home.

Bear Tale

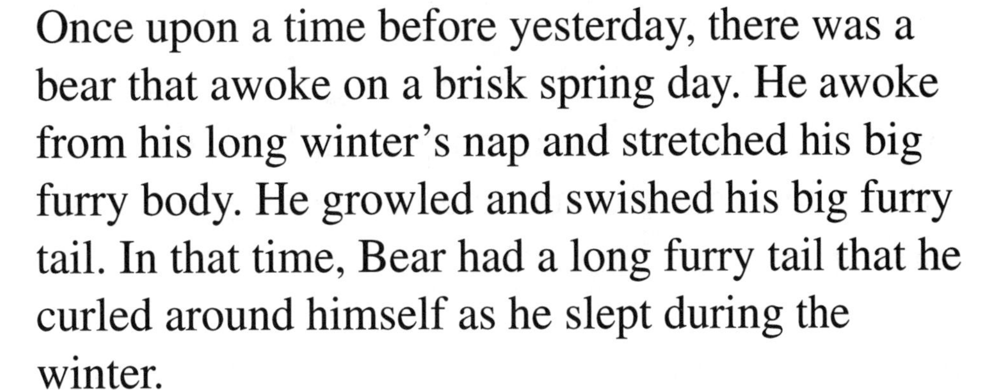
Once upon a time before yesterday, there was a bear that awoke on a brisk spring day. He awoke from his long winter's nap and stretched his big furry body. He growled and swished his big furry tail. In that time, Bear had a long furry tail that he curled around himself as he slept during the winter.

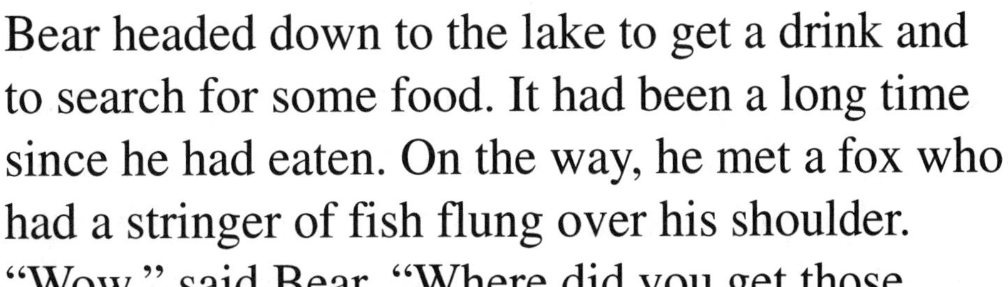
Bear headed down to the lake to get a drink and to search for some food. It had been a long time since he had eaten. On the way, he met a fox who had a stringer of fish flung over his shoulder. "Wow," said Bear. "Where did you get those fish? I am so hungry!"

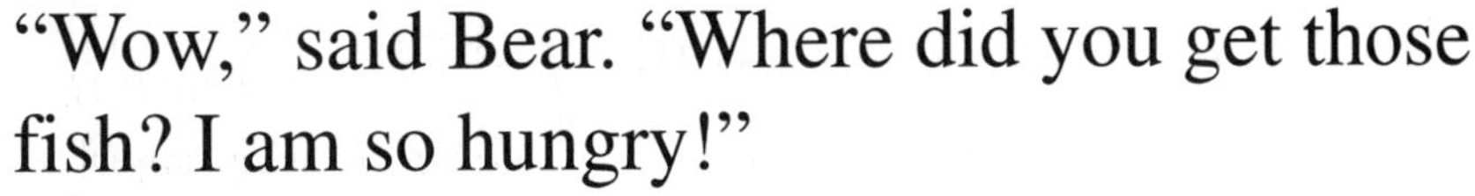
When Bear asked for one of the fish, Fox told Bear he would have to catch his own.

Fox told Bear that there were lots of fish in the lake. Bear asked, "How did you catch that mess of fish?"

Fox said, "Here is my secret and you can catch as many fish as you can eat. Pick out a spot on the ice and make a hole. Stick your long tail down in the hole and wait for the fish to bite. The longer you sit the more fish you will catch."

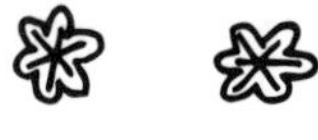

Bear Tale

Bear went out on the lake and made a hole in the ice. He stuck his tail down in the hole and waited for the fish to bite. He felt a nip on the end of his tail and then another nip and another nip and another nip.

Bear became greedy and decided to sit longer so he could get more fish than Fox.

Bear sat a long time and couldn't feel anything nipping at his tail. Since he was so hungry he decided to pull his tail out of the water and have a fish feast. Bear tried to stand up and pull his tail but it would not come out. He pulled harder and harder. He pulled as hard as he could. Snap! His tail broke off because it was frozen solid under the ice. And that is why to this day Bear has a stumpy tail!

Questions

Was Bear tricked by Fox?

Was Bear greedy?

How do you think Bear goes fishing today?

Bear Tale Song

(Sing to *Are You Sleeping?*)

Sleepy Bear, Sleepy Bear,
Time to wake up; time to wake up.
Springtime has arrived; springtime has arrived.
You can see; you can see.

Let's go fishing; let's go fishing,
Time to eat; time to eat.
Catch a mess of fish; catch a mess of fish.
Dinner time, dinner time.

Ice on the lake, ice on the lake,
Don't be greedy; don't be greedy.
Fishing with your tail, fishing with your tail.
Fox fooled you; Fox fooled you.

Kid Fun

Sing this song and make a tape recording to play back in a story area. Provide a bear and fox puppet.

Fox Jug Puppet

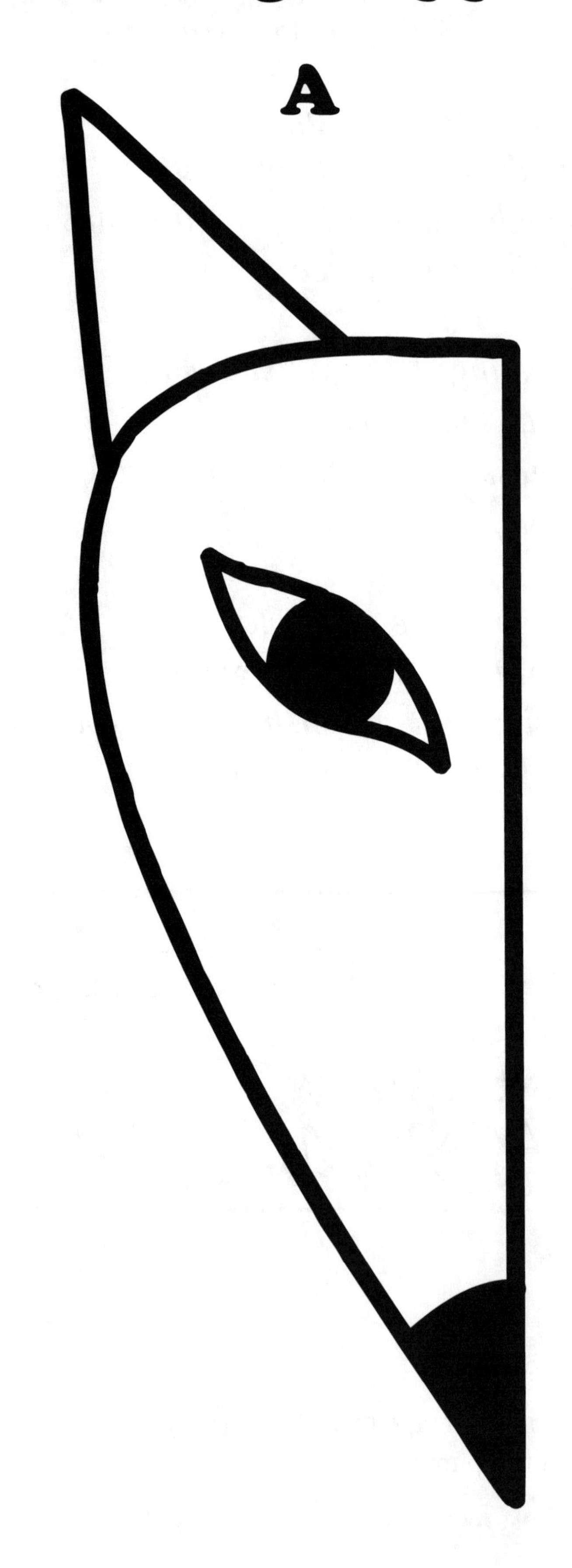

Fox Jug Puppet

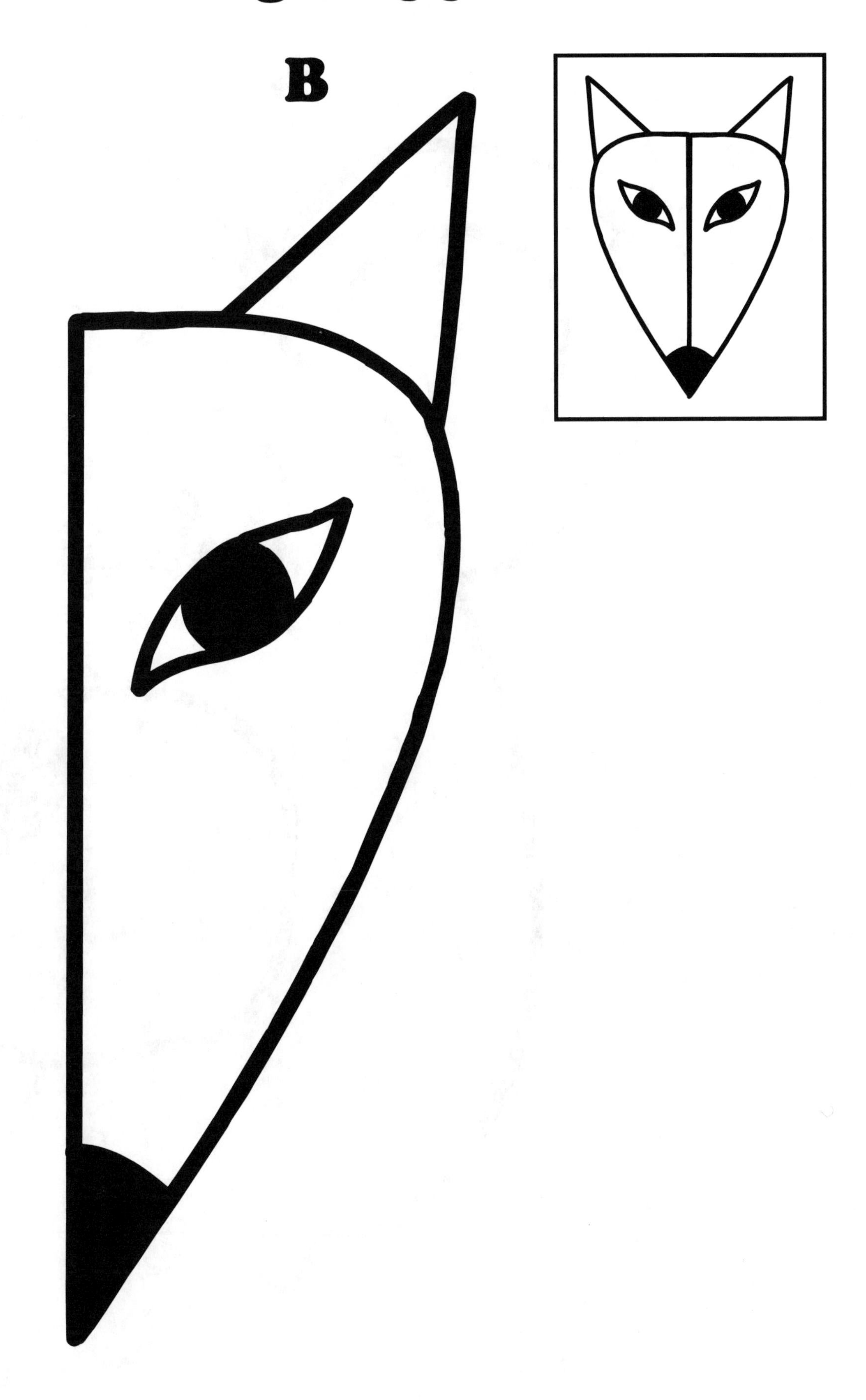

Papa Bear Jug Puppet

Papa Bear Jug Puppet

The Modern Three Bears

By Mary Jo Huff

Once upon a day before yesterday, there was a little curly-haired girl who lived in a very small town. She had a bad reputation because she was so nosy. People would fuss at her for peeking in their windows, looking in the mailbox and snooping around their yards.

Near the edge of the woods lived a bear family. Mama Bear returned home after a long day at work and asked if anyone had fixed dinner. Papa Bear and Little Bear both told her no. Mama Bear announced, “You will have to order out because I am not cooking tonight.” “Yea” said Little Bear, “Let’s have pizza.” After receiving Mama Bear’s approval, Papa Bear called the pizza delivery and ordered three pizzas. He told the pizza delivery boy to leave the pizzas on the kitchen table and to take the envelope with his payment.

Mama Bear decided to change her clothes and go for a jog before dinner. Papa Bear changed into his riding suit and decided to go along on his bike. Little Bear put on his roller blades and followed behind Mama and Papa Bear.

Not too long after they disappeared into the woods, the little blonde, curly-haired girl was taking a walk. She saw the bears leave their house. This was her chance to see what was inside the Bears’ house. Just as she turned the corner by their house, a funny-looking car with screeching tires pulled into the driveway and a strange-looking person jumped out. The boom box was rocking the car.

The Modern Three Bears

He entered the back door and the little girl crept up to the side window to see what he was doing inside. The strange looking young man took the envelope with the money and put it in his pocket. He then opened up some red leather squares and took out three pizza boxes and left them on the kitchen table.

The strange looking young man bopped out the back door and screeched his tires out of the driveway. When he was out of sight, the little girl went to the back door and turned the knob. The door was open and she went inside.

She found three pizza boxes on the table and opened the first and largest pizza box. She swiped her fingers through the topping and then licked her fingers. "YUK, it is an anchovy pizza." She then opened the second pizza box and it had mushrooms and onions and smelled really bad. "YUK, I don't like onions." Then she opened the smallest pizza and it was her favorite, pepperoni and double cheese. "YUM! YUM! YUM!" She ate the whole pizza.

Then the snoopy little girl walked into the family room and found the bear's CD players. She turned on Papa Bear's CD player but she did not like his country western music. Then she put on Mama Bear's smaller headphones but her music was too classical for the little girl. Next she put on Little Bear's small headphones and began to dance around the room. This was her kind of music. Round and around she danced.

The Modern Three Bears

After dancing for a while, the little girl was tired and wanted to lie down. She climbed up the stairs and found the bears' bedroom. She jumped in the biggest bed, but it would not stop moving. It was a waterbed and she was getting sick from the motion. She rolled out of the big bed and hopped on the cute little ruffled and lace bed. This bed was too cutesy for her taste, so she jumped on the littlest bed. This bed had a plaid bedspread with lots of animals and soft pillows. She nestled down and turned on the videotape that was in the VCR. Wow! This was a movie she had wanted her mom to get at the local video store. She nestled down in the pillows and fell sound asleep.

The three bears returned from their adventure in the woods. Mama Bear took off her jogging jacket, Papa Bear took off his headband and wrist band and Little Bear removed his roller blades. When the bears saw the pizzas on the table, they were ready to eat. Papa opened his pizza and said, "Someone has been messing with my pizza." Mama Bear opened her pizza box and said, "Someone has been messing with my pizza and it is cold and smelly." Little Bear opened his pizza box and cried, "Someone has been messing with my pizza and it is all gone." (Little Bear begins to cry.) Papa Bear said, "There is someone in this house. I can smell them. Let's go find out who is here!"

The three bears went into the family room and Papa Bear said, "Someone has been messing with my CD player." Mama Bear said, "Someone has been messing with my CD player and they left it on." Little Bear said, "Someone has been messing with my CD player and they broke my headphones." (Little Bear begins to cry.) Papa Bear said, "Let's keep looking. I can smell someone for sure."

The Modern Three Bears

The three bears climbed the stairs. When they reached the top Papa Bear turned and told Mama and Little Bear to be real quiet. The three bears tiptoed into the bedroom and Papa Bear said, "Someone has been in my bed. It is still moving." Mama Bear said, "Someone has been in my bed too and messed up my ruffles and lace." Little Bear whispered. "Come quick, there is someone in my bed." The three bears recognized the little nosey girl from down the street and decided to teach her a lesson.

The three bears gathered around the bed and on the count of three they growled as loud as they could growl. (one, two, three GROWL) The little girl woke up, saw the bears, screamed and jumped off the bed. She ran down the stairs, through the family room and kitchen and out the back door.

The nosey little girl had learned a lesson for sure and never bothered anyone in that town again.

Use Papa Bear Jug Puppet Patterns on pages 38-39.

Mama Bear Jug Puppet

A

Mama Bear Jug Puppet

B

Baby Bear Jug Puppet

A

Baby Bear Jug Puppet

B

Toby's Big Decision

By Jerry Jindrich and Mary Jo Huff

Once upon a time, on a cool fall day, a flock of geese splashed down on the pond. It was time for the geese to gather and prepare to fly south for the winter.

"I'm not going south this year," said young Toby Goose, as he splashed in the water.

"You have to fly south for the winter, you silly goose!" said his mother as she splashed water on him.

Toby did not intend to fly south. He had decided to stay and play with his friends, Bernie Bear, Buzzy Bunny, and Freda Frog. He wanted to play all winter with his friends.

All the geese had gathered on the grassy bank of the pond, ready to start their journey South. Toby's mom said, "Time to go, Toby. Are you ready?"

"I don't want to go. I want to stay here and play with my friends."

"You may not have as much fun as you think you will. All the animals act differently in the winter."

"Aw, Mom, we'll have lots of fun!"

Toby's mom looked at him sadly and flew off with the other geese. Toby watched as the geese flapped and honked their way into the sky. They quickly formed a big V and flew out of sight.

He was a little sad, but a familiar voice said, "Hello, Toby. Aren't you flying south for the winter?" It was Bernie Bear.

"I'm not going south this year," said Toby. "I'm going to stay here and play with my friends. We're going to have a good time."

Toby's Big Decision

Bernie asked Toby if he wanted to stay with his family during the winter. The cave was a nice warm place to stay for the winter, but Bernie asked Toby what he would do while his family hibernated.
"While you what?" asked Toby.

"We have to hi-ber-nate," said Bernie Bear. "That means we'll have a nice, long snooze until spring gets here."

"But I'm not sleepy," said Toby. "I want to play all winter, not hi-ber-nate."

I'll go see Buzzy Bunny. Have a nice... er... hibernation."

Bernie Bear said, "See you in the spring, Toby!"

Toby flew across the pond to find Buzzy Bunny.

Buzzy popped up out of a hole in the ground and said, "Hi, Toby! I thought all the geese were flying south today."

"Everyone else did," said Toby, "but I chose to stay here so I could play with Bernie Bear and you and Freda Frog."

"That's great," said Buzzy, "but where will you stay and what will you eat? He said this while munching on some clover. "I bet my Mom would let you stay here with us. Come on in and we'll ask her."

Buzzy hopped into his hole. Toby forgot for a moment that he was a goose and tried to hop in head first right behind Buzzy. But geese are bigger than bunnies, so there was Toby with his head and long neck down in the rabbit hole, his webbed feet up in the air and his body stuck in the opening.

The bunnies hopped out of a different hole and pulled Toby loose. Toby could see that he wouldn't fit in the Bunny family's house.

Toby's Big Decision

"I guess I'll go over and see if Freda Frog is home," said Toby. "I'm sure she doesn't live in a hole. Maybe I can stay with her family for the winter."

"I hope you find a place to stay," said Buzzy. "We could have some fun. My Mom lets me play outdoors on sunny days in the winter as long as the fox isn't around."

Toby's eyes got very big. "What fox?" he asked.

"There's a red fox that lives up in the hills," said Buzzy, "but in the winter he sneaks around here trying to catch birds and bunnies for his supper."

"But I'm a bird and you're a bunny," said Toby.

"That's why I can only play outside a little in the winter," said Buzzy, "And my Mom and Dad have to watch me while I'm playing."

"I don't think winter's going to be much fun at all," said Toby, and he waddled down to the pond and plopped in for a little swim. Toby paddled around quietly in a circle for a while, wondering if staying here for the winter was a big mistake.

Kerplunk! A big splash startled Toby and a big green face bobbed up out of the water. It was Freda Frog.

"Hi, Toby," croaked Freda. "Why aren't you flying South?"

"I wanted to stay here and play with you and Buzzy Bunny and Bernie Bear. But the Bear family's going to sleep all winter and the Bunnies live in a hole I can't fit into and the Fox might eat them if they come out to play."

"You could stay with me and my family," said Freda, "if you don't mind covering up with mud for the winter to keep your skin nice and moist."

Toby's Big Decision

"You mean you don't hop and play during the winter?" asked Toby.

"No, the pond freezes over. It's too cold and I don't like hopping on ice — makes me shiver! And there aren't many bugs to eat in the winter either. If I could fly like you, I'd be flying way down south where the water's nice and warm in the winter."

Toby was having second thoughts about not flying south for the winter. He looked up and saw a single, familiar-looking goose flying toward him.

"Mom!" he said. "I thought you were gone."

Mrs. Goose splashed down beside him and explained that the flock of geese had flown only as far as the next pond.

"I came back to see who you would be staying with during the winter."

"I want to fly south with you, Mom. I don't think I want to live here during the winter. My friends will be sleeping in a cave or staying in a hole in the ground or covering themselves with mud. Those things aren't much fun for a goose."

Mrs. Goose gave Toby a little hug and a kiss and they flew off together to the next pond to join the other geese for the big trip south.

Toby Goose Jug Puppet

Refer to and use the Bear Jug Puppet Patterns on pages 38-39.

Toby Goose Jug Puppet

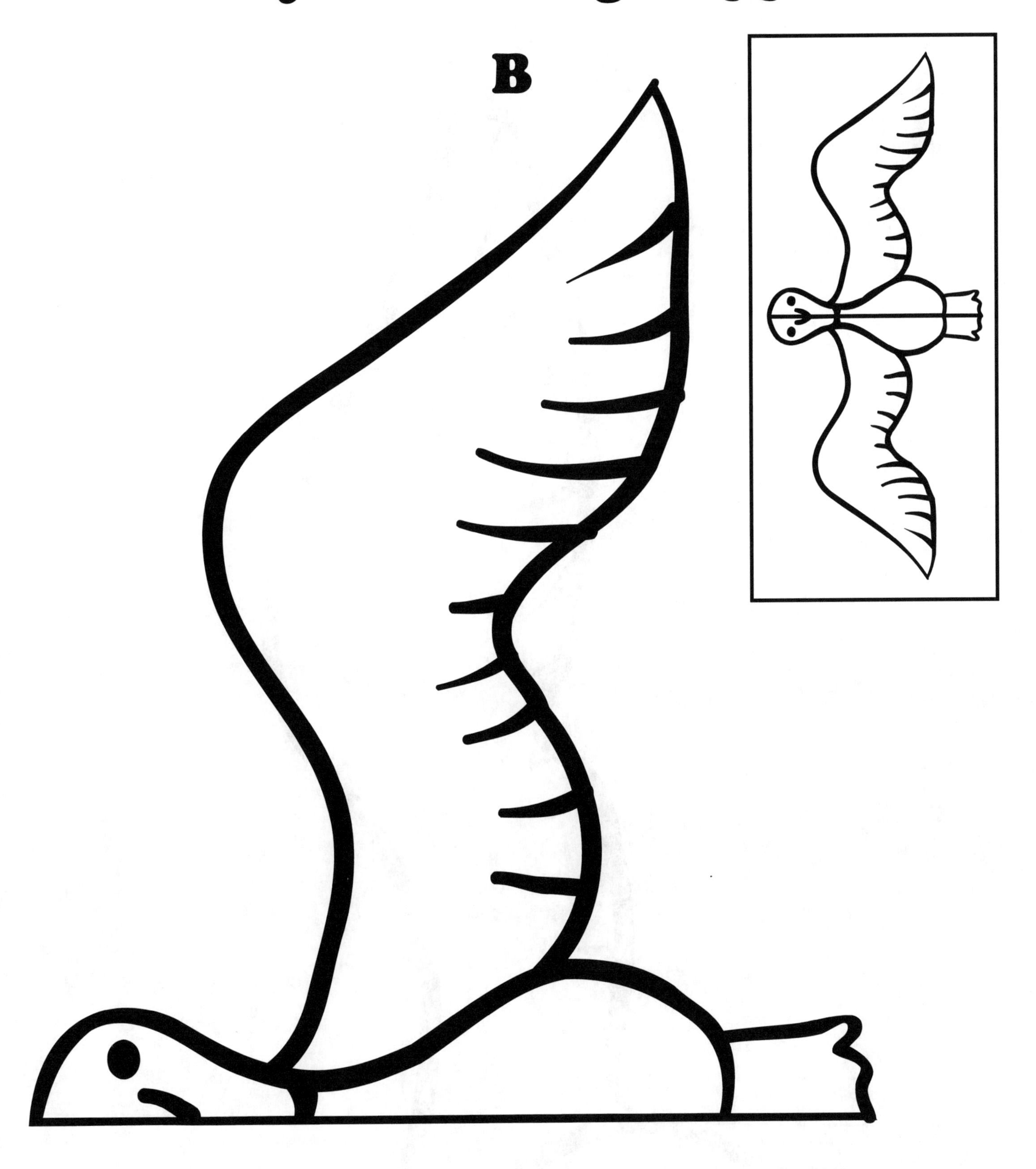

Mama Goose Jug Puppet

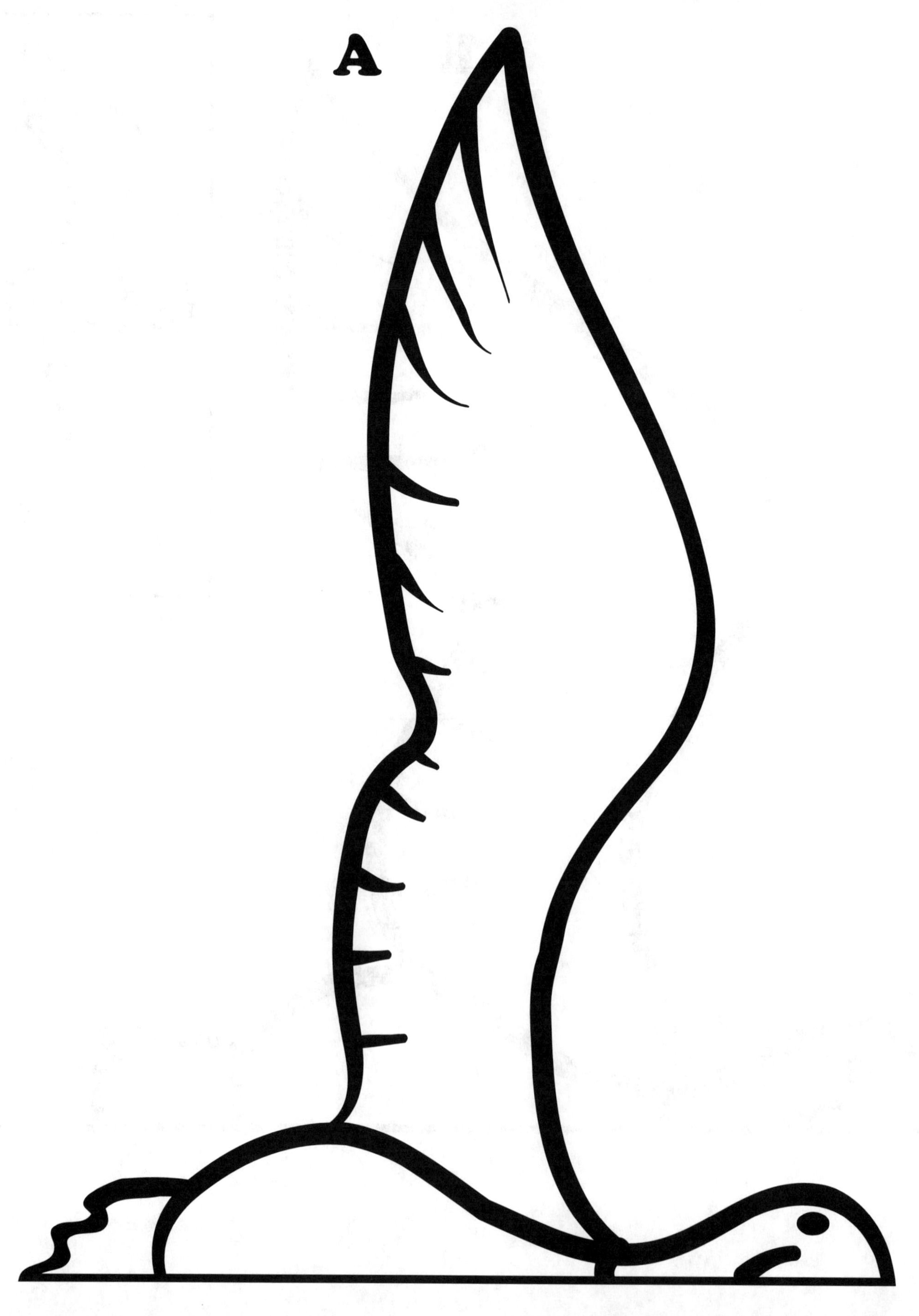

Mama Goose Jug Puppet

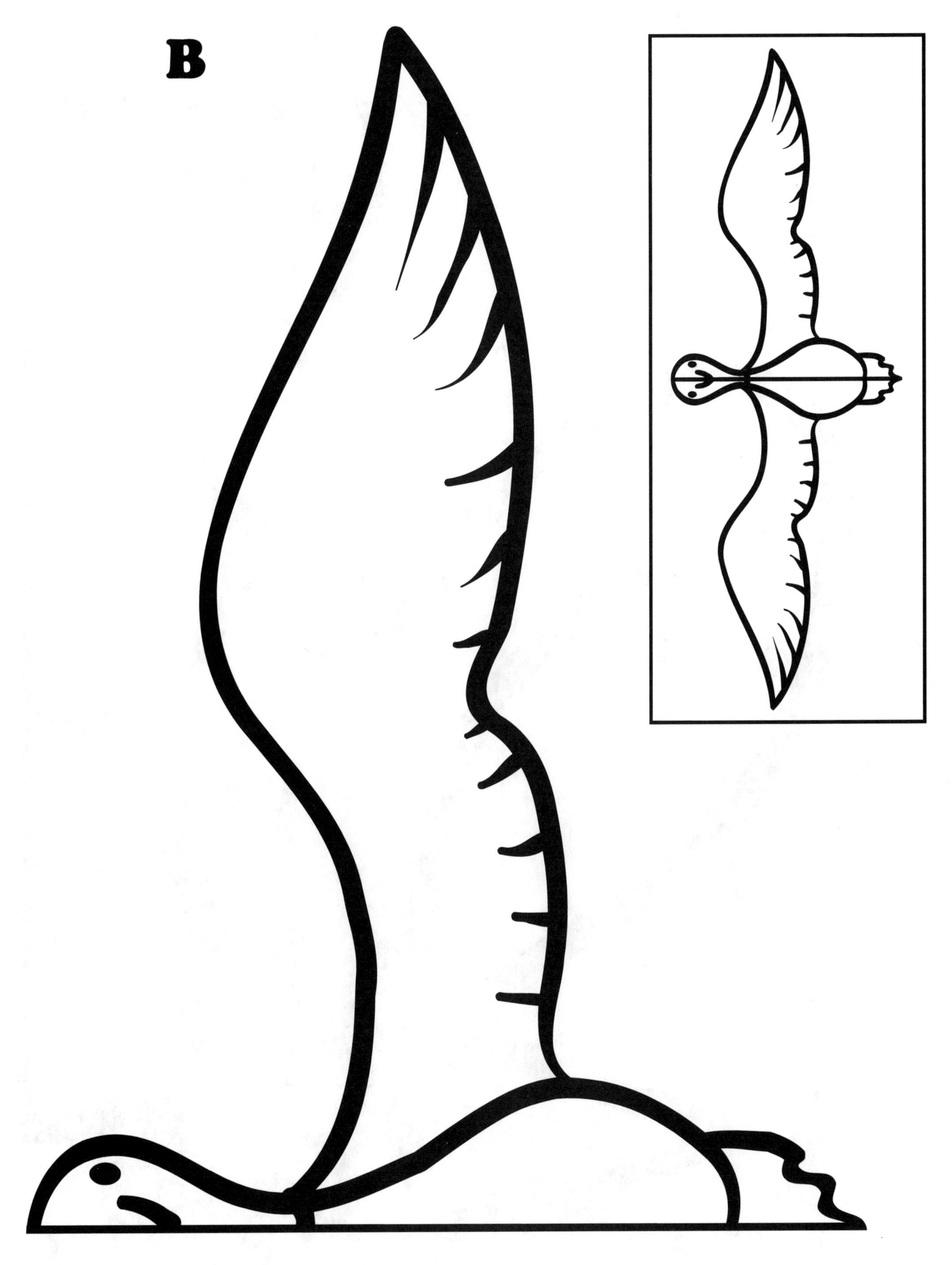

Frog Jug Puppet

Frog Jug Puppet

Rabbit Jug Puppet

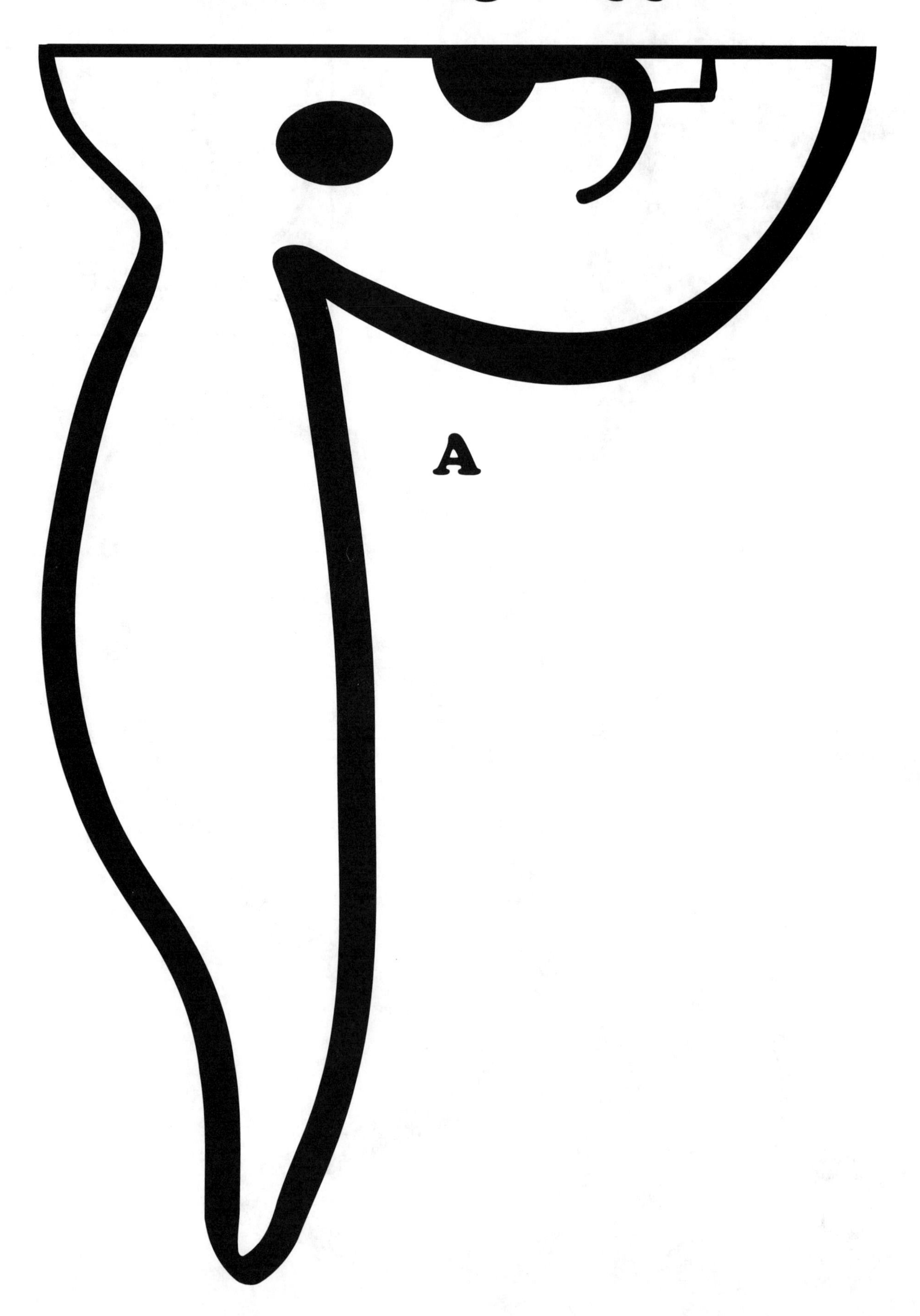

Rabbit Jug Puppet

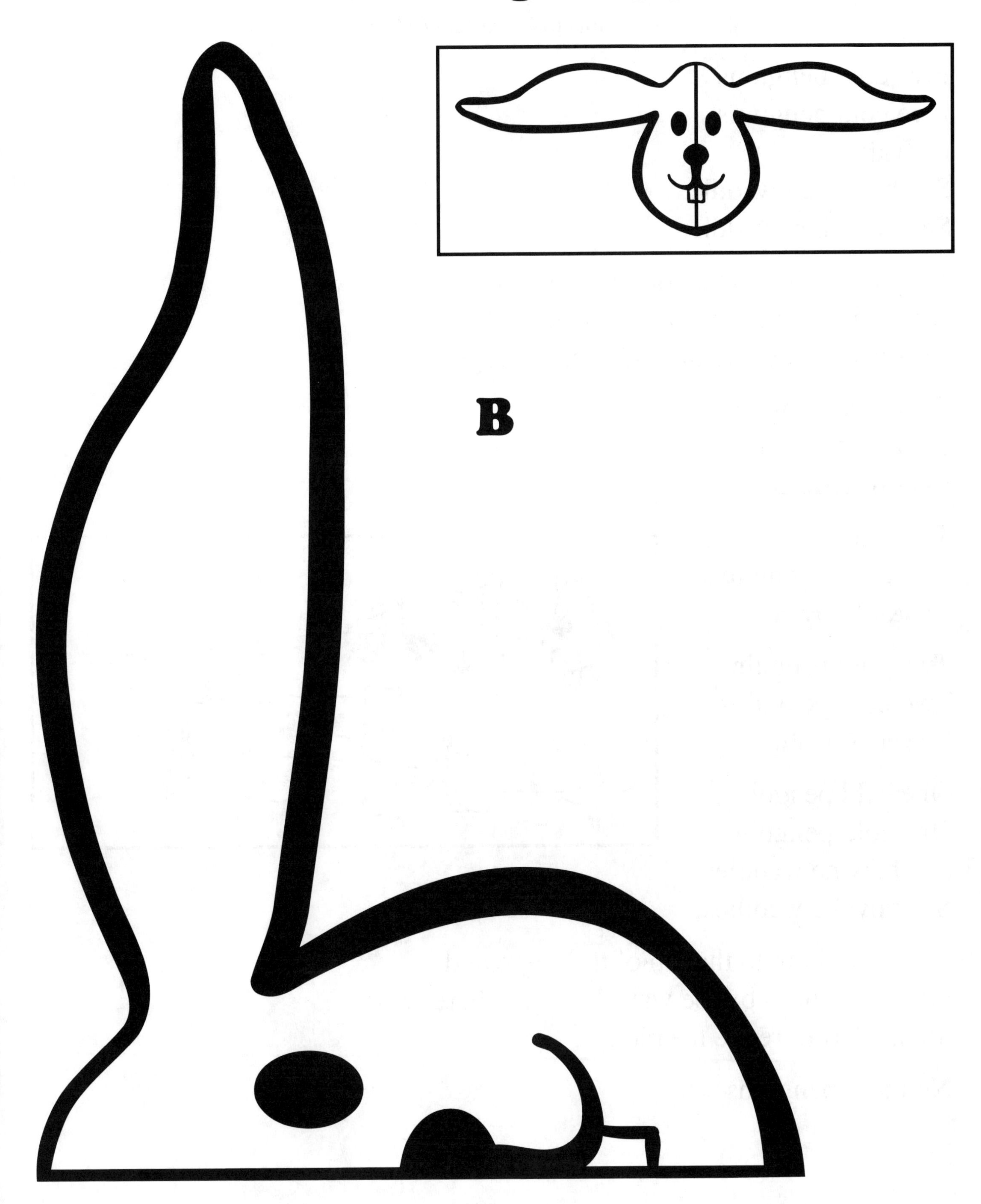

Five Cold Penguins

(Sing to *Three Blind Mice*)

Five cold penguins
Five cold penguins
Refrain
See how they waddle.
See how they waddle.

They all ran up to the top of the ledge.
One jumped right in by the water's edge.
He swam away and they said this pledge.

Four cold penguins
Four cold penguins
Repeat Refrain

Three cold penguins
Three cold penguins
Repeat Refrain

Two cold penguins
Two cold penguins
Repeat Refrain

One cold penguin
One cold penguin
See how he waddles.
See how he waddles.

He ran and ran to the top of the ledge and jumped right in by the water's edge. There was no one left to recite the pledge.

No more penguins.

Penguin Jug Puppet

Note: This pattern can be taped inside a half-gallon jug. Or split the pattern and tape and cut on the outside. Cut five penguin jug puppets to go with the Five Cold Penguins.

Winter Tales

Forest, Heather, *A Big Quiet House* (August House, 1996)

Brett, Jan, *Annie and the Wild Animals* (Trumpet Club Publishing, 1985)

Moulton, Mark Kimball, *A Snowman Named Bob* (Lang Books, 1999)

Climo, Shirley, *Cobweb Christmas* (HarperCollins, 2001)

Rosales, Melodye Benson, *Leola and the Honeybears* (Scholastic, 1999)

London, Jonathan & Sylvia Long, *Liplap's Wish* (Scholastic, 1994)

Beer, Hans de, *Little Polar Bear* (North-South Books, 1987)

Martin, Bill Jr., *Polar Bear, Polar Bear, What Do You Hear?* (Henry Holt, 1991)

Sams, Carl R. II & Jean Stoick, *Stranger in the Woods* (Edco Publishing, 2000)

Bodkin, Odds, *The Christmas Cobwebs*. (Harcourt, 2001)

Chapman, Jane, *The Emperor's Egg* (Candlewick Press, 1999)

Thury, Fredrick, *The Last Straw* (Charlesbridge, 1998)

Magee, Wes & Linda Hennessy, *The Legend of the Raggedy Boy* (Arcade Publishing, 1992)

Weedn, Flavia and Lisa, *The Little Snow Bear* (Cedco Publishing Co., 1998)

Winter Tales

Christiansen, Candace, *The Mitten Tree* (Fulcrum Publishing, 1997)

Pomerantz, Charlotte, *The Mousery* (Harcourt Brace, 2000)

Wood, Audrey, *The Napping House* (Harcourt Brace, 1984)

Moss, Miriam, *The Snow Bear* (Dutton Books, 2001)

Repchuk, Caroline, *The Snow Tree* (Penguin Books, 1996)

Fleming, Denise, *Time to Sleep* (Henry Holt, 2000)

Shecter, Ben, *When Will the Snow Trees Grow?* (HarperCollins, 1993)

Matthews, Caitlin, *While the Bear Sleeps* (Barefoot Books, 1999)

Schachner, Judith Byron, *Willy and May* (Penguin Books, 1995)

Tryon, Leslie, *Yours Truly, Goldilocks* (Simon & Schuster, 1998)

National Storytelling Network and other web sites

www.storynet.org
www.youthstorytelling.org
www.storytellin.com
www.rivertownstorytellers.com
www.meddybemps.com
www.ms_creations.com

Storytelling Resources

Mary Jo Huff, the author of many books from Monday Morning is available for Keynotes, Workshops, Storytelling Presentations, and Family Nights.
Contact her at 800-213-0527
E-mail: mjohuff@att.net
www.storytellin.com

Resources available at www.storytellin.com

"Loop"–The Velcro compatible material
"Hook"–Used for all storytelling items on the Loop material
Storytelling Apron–Velcro type material for storytelling
Story Bands–Storytelling tool for "Kid Fun"
Used for dramatic play
Commercial "Peepers"–Great language tool for retelling stories
Peeper Power–Learn how to use Peepers
Storyboard Felt Story Characters & CD
"Varmint"–Mr. Mascot and other puppet friends
CDs written & recorded by Mary Jo Huff

Jerry Jindrich, the illustrator of this book, is the master of a special web site.
www.meddybemps.com

This free web site is for teachers, young children and their parents. You can read, play and learn at this popular site. Meddybemps.com is great fun, written and illustrated in Jerry's incomparable style, accessible via the internet and the best of all, it's free!